Embrace

the Hideous Immaculate

Published by Raw Dog Screaming Press
Bowie, MD
First Edition

Editor: Stephanie Wytovich
Cover and interior illustrations: Steven Archer
Book design: Jennifer Barnes

Printed in the United States of America

ISBN: 978-1-935738-64-0

Library of Congress Control Number: 2014938263

www.RawDogScreaming.com

Embrace
the Hideous Immaculate

Poetry by

Chad Hensley

RAW DOG
SCREAMING
PRESS

Dedication

For Carey Edwina Hodges.

Contents

Introduction: Singing Ye Dark Songs

W. H. Pugmire

In an age that seems increasingly unpoetic, it is refreshing to come across a book that is the authentic thing, a collection of poems that are original and effective. Chad Hensley's poems are the real thing, songs of traditional horror, of modern surreal threats to sanity, glances at social injustice. They are the visions, primarily, of a Southern Man, in which one can hear the stridulation of cicadas and suck the air of a humid Mississippi night. But we are introduced to other realms of troubled dream, of ageless horror. We dance upon the classic sod of daemonic cemeteries, and bleed in pits where our mortal liquid spills into waiting orifices. We struggle with the agony of birth, "From a womb of darkness/Into a world of shadows," and we shudder beneath the multitudinous wings of death, where we decay, withered, dry and rotting, buried.

Fable, myth and legend have inspired our poet, as have other masters of horror such as H. P. Lovecraft. An initiation to the Outside is summoned in "The Call," a poem that is classically Lovecraftian and evocative; and a cousin to "The Outsider" wanders the dense woods of birthright, "while twilight cracks/with shadowed night." In "Nethermost Cavern" we have distinct echoes of Lovecraft's haunting tale of Kingsport, "The Festival," beautifully expressed in bewitching poetry.

For me, poetry best succeeds when it is as beautiful as it is dark and haunting. In this collection, we are assaulted by waves and waves of gorgeous, imaginative imagery, in scintillating language. Indeed, the language of poems such as "Gautier Ghost Story" and "The Night-Child's

Wardrobe are so fine that one cannot help but whisper them aloud so as to better drink in the beauty and innovation of their language.

I relish this collection, and will return to it. The only thing one can hope for is that Chad will turn his unique imagination to a new collection of weird fiction, stories written by one who has a remarkable style.

Grotesque Statue

Walking through thronged streets
I chanced to peer up
Observing half-hidden statues.

Stone gothic gargoyles glared—
Backs perpetually bent,
Faces twisted in hideousness.
Crouched on cracked cathedral tops
They stared, mocked.

That night I dreamed of gargoyles—
Gray serpentine eyes, and taloned claws.
They clutched me, purposefully peering
Atop an ancient church
As my skin turned to stone.

They departed and I saw
The face of the statue.

I awoke to the sound of heavy wings beating
And in the shallow moonlight
I laughed silently at the city below me.

Embrace the Hideous Immaculate

Mortal Remains II

In the moonlight
What shapes run
That we cannot see,

Our eyes passing
Over them with the ignorance of reason.
Only drunken old men and sleepy children

Glimpse something
Dancing in the fields at midnight or
Shimmering in the darkness just outside the window,

But, perfectly good explanations
Always turn up in the morning
As soon as the corpses are found.

At night I play

Under leafless thorny limbs clawing skyward
The bare sinuous branches
Wave against the wind
And, often, I imagine
The trees become a sea of writhing black tentacles
But the morning sun falls
Only on the forest
Though, sometimes, bleached infant bones
Are nestled in the highest trees.

Nocturnity

On her knees
The unclean virgin flicks her tongue
At the wreaths of dried flowers
Flung upon the upturned earth.
Anxious for the rotting
She begins to burrow.
Below, empty eyelids open.
Livid, festered limbs lay
Distraught at the darkness
Silently awaiting
The hideous immaculate.

Last Embrace

I dance with my lover,
Continuously whirling and turning.
She leads me,
Pulling me along,
Mesmerizing me with
Her sunken, sparkling
Blue eyes that anticipate.
Her cascading hair,
The color of decayed bones,
Dangles in my eyes, teasing.
Though I tire I will wait
To take her.
Eventually, lust will force
Me to lay with her
Forever.

Church Bizarre

I was born too late:

Never to see
Plump, round priests passing
Dead peasants rotting
Covered with rats
On a dirt road.

Never to feel
The rising heat
From burning rusted iron brands
Poked into an old man's arm
As he shouts to an inquisitor
That their god was his.

Never to hear
The screams of a pale-skinned girl
As her flesh sizzles and falls
From the blazing stake she is tied to
While surrounded by hooded men
Dressed in black.

Now, I can only touch
The knob to change the channel
As children shoot machine guns in Israel
While the pope passes, waving to
Filthy crowded streets in some city
Whose name I cannot pronounce.

Birthright

I wander deep in dense woods
while twilight cracks
with shadowed night.

Beckoning branches lead
to a mold-covered crypt
greasy from a thousand uses.

Cold, colossal stone doors open,
receiving my touch.

Weary, I lie with my ancestors
and the doors close.

Awakening, my family initiates me—
stripping the flesh from my bones
I join them.

Festival of Stigma Martyrs

When I was a child
Forced to attend church
I would stare at the adults
Waiting with open mouths
To eat the flesh and drink the blood
Of a body (I was told) that
Died two thousand years ago
In a faraway place.

Now, I watch television:
In the Middle East
Mounds of bodies pile up
Around holy warriors.
White-hooded Americans
Raise burning crosses high
Laughing at their head-shaven children
Marching in black soldier boots
Saluting long dead German leaders.
And the pope continues resting,
Waiting for another parade and
The crowd that will gather
To receive communion.

Embrace the Hideous Immaculate

Necrotivity

Weary are the bones beneath the flesh.
Anxious are they for the withering of skin
And rotting of organs they have been forced to embrace.
They lust to be placed between velvet and lace
Buried under mounds of upturned earth
Safely concealed within concrete walls.
Where they can clack to each other
In the bitter, sweet silence.

Nocturne

Her eyes are fetid black whirlpools
Continually churning, bottomless.
Her breath is thick, stagnant air
Choking the living.
Her lips are livid tendrils
Longing to entwine warm flesh.
Her tongue is a bloated leech
Hungering eternally.
Her heart is an open grave
Greedily gathering the dead.

Embrace the Hideous Immaculate

Silent Brood

In a small town
shadows breed
like whispered gossip.

The night tongues
Form festered shapes,
Warm flesh safely sleeping.

Morning finds only
another missing body
has turned up on the road.

Chad Hensley

The vampire witch boy

(for Go Nagai)

has a name that cannot be pronounced.
A cross-eyed hat sits on top of his mop of orange hair mumbling
like a bellowing bassoon in slow motion, spitting spells at random.
The boy's bushy giant eyebrows wave in the air like twitching insect antennas.
His right hand holds a wooden wand with a golden head
spraying spiraling streams of incandescent fire.
Above a sea of abandoned apartment complexes,
he hovers like a cartoon fairy
kicking at the air like a scolded child, heavy boots on his small feet.
For effect, two sharp teeth protrude from his perpetual smile,
twinkling in the moonlight as he laughs.
The sound of ghost children echoes off the walls of an empty school.
On the playground, two monstrous centipedes grow from the shoulders of
An emaciated man, oily, segmented coils entwining his jaundiced body.
He taunts the boy, arthropod mouths chittering with poisoned hunger.
Deeper in the urban darkness, other misshapen deformities lumber forward
howling in frustration.
Heedless of the tentacled shadows congealing in the broken windows
around him, the vampire witch boy laughs louder, diving straight down
into the melee,
the souls of his classmates roaring with approval,
watching from beneath the school yard, bodies drained and broken.

Embrace the Hideous Immaculate

Listen

Some say
the voice of Death is

like the gnashing of wolve's jaws
gulping muscle meat greedily

like large leathery black wings
flapping upon midnight winds

like brittle fingernails
scraping frozen cracked stone.

But I have heard
only a whisper

drifting through skeletal branches
clawing at a bloated moon

as crushed amber leafs
settle upon a silent mound of upturned earth.

A View of Videodrome Godflesh

As I child
I went to church alone
And sat in silence
While the pastor spoke.
Often his words
Made me think
Of my parents
Hatred for each other
And myself.

After service
I walked home
And turned on
The television
Before the screams
Of my mother began
As father shouted
Slurred words
While he struck her.

One Sunday afternoon
I saw a movie
Where a young boy
Became a preacher.
He grew up, moved
His congregation
To a place called Guyana.
Built a new Eden,
A town and temple

Embrace the Hideous Immaculate

For his people.
Slept with every
Woman (or boy) he wanted.
But the world wanted
His holy city
(or so he said)—
Ordered his congregation
To take communion
And drink poisoned Kool-Aid.
Then he shot himself in the head.

From the corner of my room
I can see the television.
Every day I watch
Waiting for the movie
To start again
So I can see
How I fucked up the first time.

Big Island Sunset

From the safety of my high-rise balcony,
The tropic resort has become prehistoric:

The beach is an expanse of sparkling black sand
Ground from shards of lava
Each sickle-sharp and jagged as broken glass.
Chest-high viridian waves crash against the petrified coastline,
The receding ocean as loud as the scraping claws of an army of giant insects.

An enormous hawksbill sea turtle pulls itself out of the tidal waters,
Corded muscles covering flipper-like arms,
Barreled shell bigger than a fifty-five-gallon steel drum,
Obsidian beak glistening wickedly
With turtle spit and tiny encrusted barnacles.

Below me, the brackish waters of an anchialine pool bubble.
Shrimp the size of squirrels skip across the oily surface,
Their broad, hooded carapaces curved
Like the rusted heads of medieval weapons.

The cinderblock surfaces of the balcony fuse into a monolith
Covered with petroglyphs of dancing six-legged lizards.
Weathered rattan furniture reweaves itself
Into eight-foot tall tiki statues,
Yellow flames leaping from cavernous eyes.
Carved hands clench harpoons and twisted vines
That burn with sparkling green phosphorescence.

Embrace the Hideous Immaculate

A stocky, squatting tiki points to the sinking sun,
Raises a huge seashell to splintering wooden lips
And a deep bellow echoes through the night air.

Far out at sea, the ancestral voices of the tribal dead answer.
Clouds brood around an elephantine moon.
Leviathan-sized shadows rise and lumber shoreward.

Necklaces of sweet-smelling, bright colored flowers
Drop around my neck
For, as the guest of honor at tonight's luau,
I am to be eaten.

Chad Hensley

Stranded in Mississippi

On a sweaty summer night, I stroll
A pock-marked stretch of Highway 90,
Dodging potholes and a dead possum,
The heady scent of fresh cut grass and wild onions
Lingering still.

Magnolias sprawl skyward,
Not really happy with the remnants of revenants in their soil,
Limbs scoliotic and cataracted,
Unable to decide which way
To reach for a heaven
That's surely hidden somewhere just above the domed slate of darkness.

Stooped by the roadside
An old black man, shoeless and skeletal,
Collects desiccated teeth of Civil War soldiers.
Pushes bits of bone into his cavernous gums for an enduring smile.
He'll walk bounteous miles to the French Quarter,
Give his Cheshire grin as a gift to the Chicken Man
For a voodoo ritual in Lafayette cemetery
Sure to speckle his robin-egg eyes for a hundred more years
With rumblings beneath venerable earth and
Antediluvian voices that still remember forgotten festivals of jubilant days.

Over the cooling pavement
Rusting pickup trucks roar
Like runaway trains in heat,
Back windshields covered
With stickers of Confederate flags and fish symbols.

Embrace the Hideous Immaculate

Inside filthy cramped cab darkness,
A mass of bloodshot eyes glow maniacal.
Clawed hands darting toward the gun rack
At the slightest sound of honking.

Throat parched for companionship,
I stop at the Super Walmart,
Looking for a Dixie peach in pigtails and cut-offs.
I find obese zombies shuffling through the aisles on electric carts,
Flabby skin flaps sloughing off in great oily folds,
Fresh Dead Sea scrolls for future generations.

In an adjacent pasture
Decapitated clansmen whistle for their bodies,
Ghostly white hoods whirling in the wind like discarded laundry,
Trails of rising steam.

Back on the tarmac,
All I've got to show for my travels
Is a dime bag of Mexican dirt weed and a pocket full of change,
Hoping for a high plains drifter,
A mockingbird's song somewhere in the distance ahead of me.

Chad Hensley

Diablo Musica

Beneath a shimmering horizon of sun,
Rows of cramped stalls wind like rattlesnakes.
Vendors shout in ancient languages thick with desert grit and dead gods,
Rough hands and pocked faces burned brown by blistered centuries.
In the gutted belly of the market, half-hidden in oblong shadows,
Sits a large ceramic bulldog with a wide, lopsided grin.
Beneath bulging, cinereous eyes a fat toad-like tongue lolls
Out the corner of a cavernous mouth,
Tiny chips in the weathered paint of plaster-black jowls.
Large horseflies with iridescent eyes
Loop-de-loop in the sweltering heat around the statue
But never land near
The twitching, hairless carcass covered with scurrying brown scorpions.
Rivulets of stagnant blood pool below on the dirt floor
Draining from Styrofoam chests filled with dirty ice and animal parts.
Outside, the call of the western dead howls up
With hot winds and bits of bone scattered across the infernal plains,
A monotone sound like the banter of a Tijuana DJ
Stoned on sour tequila and barbequed iguana
Mumbling something about the bodies of stupid gringos
Layered beneath the sands.

Embrace the Hideous Immaculate

Mardi Gras after Midnight

At 2 a.m. the last parade drifts
down St. Charles Avenue.

Skeletal steeds spew
black froth from their bony jowls
as they pull subterranean floats.

The riding revelers wear cowls
of scale-like, sparkling red sequins
stitched to their serpentine bodies,
faces covered by golden masks,
empty eye sockets reflecting the faces of the screaming crowd.

Gold coins thrown into the throng
burn through flesh.
Tossed small, silver toys
bite with tiny razor teeth.

But, the best catch is an obsidian goblet
for a single sip from the cup
dissolves the drinker
as the parade dissipates just before dawn.

Chad Hensley

Mexican Standoff

An hour outside of Brownsville,
A desert road winds like a rattlesnake for miles,
Weaving around cactuses, tumbleweeds, and sun-bleached cow skulls.
At a cul-de-sac, hot shimmering sands blow through
Open windows of an abandoned building, tattered curtains flapping.
In the garage, a rotting, limbless torso hangs from hooks in the ceiling,
A thousand flies and maggots feeding.
Bloody boot prints lead through the kitchen,
Empty bottles of beer and Tequila dotting the countertop.
A beautiful, blond-haired woman is roped to a chair in the center of the living room.
Her bloodshot eyes bulge with insanity,
Tiny rivers of mascara running down her cheeks.
She mumbles, mouth gagged with black electric tape,
Dirty sweat pouring down her face.
A brown-skinned man steps out of the closet in a cloud of marijuana smoke,
Eyeholes cut into the cloth of the flour sack covering his head,
Bandoleers crisscrossing his broad chest, holstered pistols at his sides.
He pulls off his mask, shadows scurrying from the empty sockets of a skull.
Screams echo back across the border
Where a mouth of broken teeth twitches
Beside the body of a migrant worker
Buried on the roadside somewhere in Texas.

Embrace the Hideous Immaculate

The Jackpot

The Big Easy
Is what they call the new casino.
I went there once and watched
An anorexic old woman with a bright yellow bouffant
Sitting in front of a slot machine,
Thin, tumored hand
Rubbing the handle up and down between pulls,
Long drags off cigarettes,
And phlegm-filled coughs.
An overweight bald man in a thrift store suit
Sat beside the woman,
Thick, brown drool running down his chin.
The corner of his mouth gnawed at a cigar butt
As he gazed glass-eyed.
Above the couple,
A tall black man in a white tuxedo
Looked down from a balcony balustrade,
Black top hat high on his curved forehead.
His cloven shoes sparkled strangely in the glare of blinking neon.
He smiled to reveal a mouth of glittering gold
His right hand waved an ebony cane topped with
A sparkling, silver skull.
He nodded at me and laughed.
The sound that escaped his throat was
A multitude of slot machines simultaneously hitting the jackpot.
I turned and ran, trying to imagine money spewing everywhere.
But all I could see was
a suburb of old houses, the paint peeling,
And the rotting bone beneath.

Chad Hensley

Pilgrimage

Took a car ride
To find the Holy Land;
Where the blessed dwell.
Drove south towards Memphis.
Reached a dead god's shrine of grace
But an admission fee
Was charged at the gate
So we had to keep driving.
Not far more here
God fear'n country folk
Were happy to oblige us.
Set giant crosses on fire.
Made sure we didn't get lost.
A few white-robed sheriffs,
Fundraising by the highway,
Shook their hoods
Pointed us further on.
Down the road our car
Was forced over and
Now I fear my body
Will never be found
Buried in these woods.

Embrace the Hideous Immaculate

Gautier Ghost Story

Humid Mississippi night in mid-April
Way past late
Scratchy black woods soaked in ground fog
Slippery for miles in every direction
Thick rotten egg stench of paper mills
Almost tearing my eyes with atrophied memories.
Across milky-chocolate-bayou waters
In scabrous patches of clawing sea oats
Blue crab shadows whisper taunts
Below a hairline crack of jester moon.
Where choked marsh and caustic sand meet
Speckled with footprints
Drowned in deep gulf
Forgotten summers ago
I hit I-10, snarling tarmac
Trailing me for hours like rabid hound dogs,
Thin glaucous tint covering the land
Behind me.

Chad Hensley

The Ghost of Buena Vista

Halfway down Biloxi Beach
On the other side of Highway 90
right beneath the rising onramp
stood the Buena Vista hotel.

As a boy, I visited for a day every summer
during a science fiction convention
dropped off way early by Dad
on his way to work despite the weekend.

Waiting for the dealer's room to open
I hung out near the basement
in a tiny mildewed room
that played kung-fu films and Japanese monster movies around the clock
on a pull-down screen and classroom projector,
piles of round canisters littering the floor in the back corner
like a graveyard of tiny flying saucers,
strands of celluloid unwinding alien intestines.

My third summer at the hotel,
Under a dusk-bruised sky of purples and deep reds,
I kissed a girl on the third story balcony.
She had long hazelnut hair and skin like bars of fresh soap,
Brown eyes deep pools of molten molasses.
A warm breeze scented the cooling shadows with spice of distant oceans
and blooming honeysuckle.

She was babysitting her brother.

Embrace the Hideous Immaculate

Like an emaciated Quasimodo,
he walked as if he was humpbacked,
right hand curled to his chest,
pretending to pick lice from his body and flick it at passersby.
He stalked the halls,
stinging caterpillars crawling on his bare arms and shoulders.
His grades were poor, except for a perfect score in science.

In college, I returned to the hotel.
Rows of rusted chain-linked fence blocked most of the driveway,
Lower balconies overgrown with impenetrable walls of thorned vine.
Despite the huge patchwork of boards nailed over the main entrance,
a small hole led into the lobby.

Every floor was covered with broken glass,
Jagged pieces of mirrored walls reflecting
a thousand fractured images of dark hair and gleeful eyes,
shadows thrusting in the darkness,
sharp points of flashlight bouncing.

Chad Hensley

A Nasty Encounter with Roadkill

On the hot tarmac
I saw a small, furry carcass.
Empty eye sockets stared
From a flattened, hairless head.
The noonday sun had cooked the skin,
A pungent stench of soured meat and shit.
I kicked at the bloated belly,
Hoping it would burst with an army of crawling insects.
Instead, a sea of writhing tendrils unwound
Around multiple eyes
and a thousand tiny mouths
Smiled with rows of minute stiletto-like teeth.
Gibberish laughter chased me,
The mound of cartilage
Crawling on the asphalt behind.

Embrace the Hideous Immaculate

IQ Test

Broken beer-bottle teeth gnaw nervously,
Gums infected and bleeding.
Soiled, fat fingers caress
A wad of matted hair caked with semen.
Another body twitches beneath the floorboards,
Tendrils of steam coiling skyward.
From hidden camera safety
The eugenicist smiles, statistics confirmed.
Outside, flashbulb staccatos strobe-light the darkness
Behind the police swarming the woods around the house.
A mile down the road, moonlight silhouettes a hobbling, hunched form,
Pudgy hands wrapped around cooling ankles
Hoping he can get it right this time.

Chad Hensley

Something My Grandfather Taught Me

Eidetic as yesterday, I remember
Sitting on the carpet after Thanksgiving dinner,
Listening to Papa Jack ramble
Of his days toiling on the railroad,
Round, silver pocket watch clutched in his trembling, age-spotted hand
Keeping time with his tales.
Tick Tick Tick…

"Man never landed on the moon.
That's Hollywood hogwash
Born In the basement of some fancy movie studio,"
He'd say, chewing on the unraveling butt of his fat stogie,
Blowing smoke rings around the living room.
Layered underneath the sharp, acrid stench of tobacco
Something lingered on his breath;
A subtle, rancid smell, vile and grotesque,
I never could quite place.
Tick Tick Tick…

Now, every time I floss my teeth
I taste Papa Jack's breath,
Between bicuspids,
Red gums sore and bleeding.
Days ago, I'd thought I'd found
The source of the old man's mouth stench
Deep in the woods behind this house,
Rising off the rusting railroad tracks.
Purple-black bruises as big as my fist
Covered her slender body, face a pulped mass.
But when I bent down and sniffed inside

Embrace the Hideous Immaculate

I didn't smell Papa Jack's breath in her pretty, perfect mouth
Nor was it in the smooth, hairless gash between her legs.
Tick Tick Tick…

Maybe Death lives on the moon
Stinking up miles of deep crater and dust.
Sure as hell, Papa Jack's breath must be there now
Watching me drag the whore's broken body to the basement.
Piled in the corner with the others,
The reek of rotting flesh still ain't the same.
But, I know that if I keep looking,
Toiling hard over miles of iron track,
I'm sure to find the source,
Snuff it out forever or, at the very least,
Cover up the odor with corpses
Buried beneath the basement of a fancy movie studio
Somewhere in Hollywood.
Tick Tick Tick…

Chad Hensley

Dark Entry

Under a sweltering summer sun
I walk on the sidewalk
Watching insects crawl in between the cracks
Over cigarette butts and bottle caps.
Where corner pavement merges with building bricks
Web-covered crevices teem with spiders spinning egg sacks.
Above entranceways wasp nests and dirt dauber mounds
Mold into the woodwork almost unnoticed.
At sunset I hurry home for the safety of indoors.
Once inside, my room somehow seems smaller
And, if I listen, there is a clicking in the shadows.

Embrace the Hideous Immaculate

American Dream

I live in the suburbs—
Outside my house
Black kids drive new Porsches
Delivering crack door to door
As their beepers continually buzz.
At the street corner
Police sit parked in the alley
Waiting patiently
For anyone to walk past
And allow them an excuse
To exercise their golf stroke.
Down the block
The local church congregation
Lights a giant cross on fire
And throws bricks through
The windows of Semitic-owned stores.

But only on television
Have I ever seen a ghetto
Where children shoot machine guns
As they drive through the neighborhood,
Stray bullets hitting whoever they can find
And the old people sit on the front porch
Rocking slowly as they watch and sip cheap wine.

Chad Hensley

Macabre II

Birth is pain:
From a womb of darkness
Into a world of shadows.

Life is pain:
Watching transmitted tragedies
Spread reproduced misery
Through stale static light
Reflecting on numb faces
That continue to stare
And refuse to change the channel.

Death is pain:
People arrive,
Dressed in imitation melancholy black,
To walk through a twilight
Sparkling on rows of granite obituaries
And the fake flower wreaths that cover them.

Embrace the Hideous Immaculate

Harvest

As a child
At dusk I listened
To the cicada swarm
Hissing in the treetops,
They sounded like electricity
Showering sparks on the pavement.
Always, I would climb
The loudest tree.
When I reached the top
I heard only silence
Until I scampered down
And the hissing rose again.
In the morning
Tiny grotesque husks
Covered the branches.
I collected the shells
For I knew the cicada
Had left them for me.

Chad Hensley

Bedtime Story (a sonnet)

Down a cold, shadowed street a dark house stands.
Under its creaking roof a mother sits
Reading to children who whisper demands
Wishing to be scared out of their frail wits.
When she is through reading the children's tale
And several hours ago turned out the light,
The sleeping children awake, frightened pale
From dreams at the exact stroke of midnight.

They clutch their sheets staring at a shadow
Moving behind their heads on the far wall
Afraid to look across at the window
Knowing they had better not scream at all.
Soon they shall whimper themselves back to sleep
While in their room the shadow continues to creep.

Embrace the Hideous Immaculate

Hollywood Labyrinth before Sunset

Spray painted cryptic symbols cover
Every inch of brick wall.
On the sidewalks footprints smudge
Embedded marble stars
Of forgotten gods.

High priced priestesses,
Built silicone perfect,
Strut in skintight gowns of gossamer
Hurrying to their next video shrine.

Leather-clad weekend warriors
Ride custom-built, two-wheeled chariots,
Emblazoned courage
Tattooed on their biceps.

The homeless wanderer watches,
Hands and face stained asphalt,
From a cardboard castle
On the street corner.

Chad Hensley

Ancient One

Once I had a dream
Of a place
Deep in the earth—
A vast lightless cavern
Half-submerged by an archaic sea.
On the shore I wandered
In phosphorescent lichens' glow.
Black pools bubbled,
Belching acrid fumes into the air.
Stalactites dripped ochre-colored slimes.
Inland I went, drawn.
I came upon a colossal statue
Rising from a gigantic crevice.
Made of unknown metal
Its many scales shimmered.
Mesmerized I peered up.
Enormous obsidian eyes,
Surrounded by tentacles,
Gazed at me.

I awoke to the sound of waves
Lapping at a midnight shore
Waiting for shadows to rise
From the deep churning waters
And in feeble moonlight
I shall swim home.

Embrace the Hideous Immaculate

The Horde

From the roof of my apartment
I could see the skyline
Burning from multiple fires
All over the city,
Swallowing the afternoon sun
In a soot shroud.

I did nothing but watch
And return indoors and stare
At the television's close-up shots
Of flames and figures
As they shattered windows,
Smashed faces with fists and bricks,
Looted and laughed.
Surging forward
They swarmed anything
Blocking their way.

After dusk, news channels
Became entertainment.
I sat back, snorted a line of cocaine up my nose,
And swallowed another mouthful of Corona
For I wanted to be completely wasted
By the time they made it
To my street.

Chad Hensley

Whisper

Beyond the stars I wandered
Guided by the gibbous light of a horned moon.
I came upon a narrow path
Leading into the forest darkness.
Entwined by tendril shadows
I followed the trail to
An enormous mold-covered crypt.
A robed figure stood before the entrance
Beckoning me to approach.
Within the cowl I saw
Twin black whirlpools
Continually churning, bottomless.
I awoke only to the wind
Scraping at my window,
The moon staring on in silence.

Embrace the Hideous Immaculate

Abyssal Plain

In a deep forest
Skeletal branches gouge at a midnight sky
At the edge of an enormous cliff.
Down in craggy depths
Moonlight crawls over the pitted walls
Of a circle of giant obelisks
Wrapped in shadow tendrils.
Small, naked forms squat
Atop the tall, narrow modular towers.
Cold, nocturnal winds carry
Gibbering whispers of lost children
That have wandered too far.
Further below, a multitude of writhing bodies
Undulates like a single mass.
A toad-like croaking fills my ears
And I leap headfirst beckoned by my brothers.

Chad Hensley

Laugh of the Night Ocean

Waiting, I sit
On wooden planks
At the edge of a rotting pier
Watching undulating darkness
Usher in the tides.

The sky peers down
With bright burning eyes
Gazing in pity.

From nocturnal waters
Tendriled shadows emerge
Entwining the soft, warm
Flesh of my body.
Pale, succulent skin
Melts in quivering ecstasy.
Laughing hysterically,
My phosphorous liquescence
Oozes into the receding waves,
Carrying me home.

Embrace the Hideous Immaculate

Feast of Lilith

After twilight
The darkness of night
Yearns to feed
The fondling hands
And caressing tongues
Of her children.

At the stroke of midnight
Sticky, sweet pale moonlight
Seeps into her black
Womb of shadow
Forming festered
Dark shapes
Awaiting birth.

Before dawn
New-born shadows
Feed on frail mortal flesh.
Darkness then dines
On their fowl forms
And returns to sleep again.

Metamorphose

Walking at dusk
I beheld a bloated, fat moon
Bathing the earth
In a sanguine shimmer.
Far off, the sound
Of howling dogs
Broke the silence.
A tremulous fear
Fell upon me.
The incessant baying
Grew louder.
My flesh quivered
In the crimson light.
My back buckled,
Spine twisting out of shape.
My face elongated,
And with razor teeth,
I bit into the flesh of my snout.
I glared at the circle
Of beasts surrounding me.
Snarling with an adrenaline rush
Of pure insolence
I screamed into the night
And with a triumphant howl
The wolf pack roared.

Embrace the Hideous Immaculate

Mother Lilith (a sonnet)

She stares hungrily at the frigid night
Watching stark shadows caress human breasts.
Her livid tendril lips rub with delight
Waiting patiently for invited guests.

Bloated tongues slither down a thin pale throat
Sucking out every drop of precious wine.
Mewing fills the air, that of many goat.
Human legs run, hiding behind a pine.

Animal hooves imprint a mildewed ground.
A frail body falls limply to the earth.
Stale stagnant air exhales without a sound,
In silence a nocturnal womb gives birth.

Horned infant shapes squirm in jaundice moonlight.
Voices whisper of Walpurgis birthright.

Chad Hensley

A Murmur of Taunting Immortality

Twilight sifts down
On a thin trembling figure
Standing in a field of white lilies,
Her shimmering skin a milky amber.
A soft incessant wind sways
Her long auburn hair,
The moon pools
In luminescent puddles
On the flowers at her feet.
Placidly she steps
Towards me
Arms outstretched,
Her fingertips touch
My quivering chest
And I awaken.

I stand, staring
At the carved alabaster headstone.
Moonlight spills over the smooth mound
And the small roses entwining the grave.
I pick a flower—two needle thorns
Piercing my fingers.
Blood patters
To the parched ground.
From beneath my feet
Faint laughter rises.
I clench the key
In my pocket
With white knuckles
And walk away.

Embrace the Hideous Immaculate

Nethermost Cavern

In a dream I followed
A procession of cowled figures
Through a winter forest.
We came upon a staircase
Chiseled out of solid rock
Descending into the damp earth.
Feeble lantern light revealed
Narrow stone steps spiraling
Down into the darkness.
Cracked walls dripped
Foul, fluorescent fungi.
Far below I heard
The sound of lapping waters.
I beheld a vast fungous shore
Filled with giant toadstools.
Those I had followed
Joined hands upon the beach
And a sickly green flame
Spouted from the center of their circle.
In the black waters
A massive amorphous form rose
Waving tentacles into the air.
A cacophony of insane fluting began
And, with a single voice we shouted.

Chad Hensley

Initiation into the Night Forest

Night breathes cool darkness
Over the remnant stench of day
Whispering with the clicking of insect songs.
Widow mother spins
Elaborate silken tapestries.
Wolves whimper
Hungry for affection.
Beneath moist earth
Other creatures slumber
Not yet allowed to awaken.

Silently, a human child tiptoes unafraid
On feet mud-caked from wandering far.
Delighted, she sits amidst the mushrooms
Patiently awaiting he that comes
To kiss her goodnight.

Embrace the Hideous Immaculate

Ghost of the Nuclear City

Through empty streets
The withered child walks bare feet blistered
Every building abandoned to shadow.
Wandering further she finds
Packs of skeletal-thin rabid dogs,
Black froth foaming from their mouths
As they dismember rotting corpses
That appear never to have been human.
She stops to stare
At the fetid plains that plutonium burned
And listen to the wind hissing
Outside Chernobyl.

Waiting for Eternity

In the void of space
He stands shadowless,
His expressionless face watching
With ageless eyes full of stars.
An amorphous robe coils
His membranous form in pools of rippling onyx.
He stares into a cold-blue-boreal beauty
Writhing with polypous tendrils
In a sea of gibbering mouths
That laugh with the shrill voice
Of a thousand screaming newborns.

Embrace the Hideous Immaculate

Pains of the Sufferer

There is a vast city
Made of fragile infant bones
Where streets are paved with crushed skulls.
All roads lead to a fountain square
Where statues with saurian heads
Sit on bodies of six-legged dogs
That dangle mouthed organs between their legs
Jetting thick milky green ichors.

Not far from the fountain
A tower of severed spines juts skyward
Piercing the perpetually clouded night.
At the top a solemn window looks
Upon flayed flesh plains below.
Here one stands with ashen hooves
Tearing great gashes into the floor.
His arms are crossed upon his chest.
His hands bleed black gangrenous gore.
His membranous wings beat freezing winds
Prickling thick hairs along his back.
From a rigid position he cannot bend
Tied with heavy chains that never slack.
He looks upon his world learning
Nothing he wasn't taught before.
What he ponders only the dead know
Until the end of evermore.

Chad Hensley

Night Carnival

At 2 a.m. the ticket booth opens.

But get there early
The show always sells out.

Winged clowns fly
Around the colossal tent
Swooping to pick up
Members of the audience.

Midgets on giant wolves
Leap through flaming hoops
Six-inch teeth gnashing.

Bone-thin acrobats
Summersault on the center trapeze.
Spiraling to the ground
They smash into pieces,
Reform, and walk away.

Before dawn
The carnival closes
And only those
Not carried off by the performers
Feel cheated.

Embrace the Hideous Immaculate

Savings and Loan

Standing in line, waiting for my turn at a teller,
I saw an enormous obese woman in an over-sized, green windbreaker.
Her giant, pudgy hands pulled at the corners of her plastic coat,
Trying to tug it around her huge, bloated midsection with fat, flabby arms.
Her greasy hair was matted to her head like unraveling, mildewed yellow yarn.
Thick, blue blood vessels snaked around her sweaty, swollen face.
For a second, I caught a glimpse of a straight razor's gleam,
Slicing twitching tendrils from deep cavities,
Great folds of muscle and meat sloughing off beneath plastic.
She pushed squirming shapes back into her pockets,
A bulging, malignant glare returning my stare and
She quickly finished straightening her coat.
I averted my eyes, pretending not to notice
The bank teller shuffling into the vault,
Stuffing seething, severed shadows into a safety deposit box
As the woman hobbled out the glass door into the crowded street,
A wide, rotting grin on her face,
Tiny bits of flesh between her teeth, belly quivering.

Chad Hensley

Block Party

Gutter punks, full of scabbed piercings and homemade tribal tattoos,
Run through the streets.
Crowbars and combat boots shatter storefront windows.
They tag buildings with spray-painted protest slogans.
Black hoodies and red bandannas hide their dirty faces.
Like masked outlaws, their eyes sparkle with a gleeful madness.
Blue helmets, thick plastic visors pulled down, obscure the faces
Of police officers wearing gas masks, armored shirts, and plated kneepads.
Cops clench hardwood batons like spears,
Jabbing blunt ends into soft body parts.
Deputies tightly grip tiny rifles,
Indiscriminately shoot cans into the air
That hit the ground spewing a thick burning fog.
Neighborhood residents tired of the melee
Throw Molotov cocktails from rooftops,
Criss-crossed in the beams of helicopter searchlights.
Billowing clouds of tear gas roll down the street,
Spilling into open doors and back alleys
Where overturned dumpsters blaze like bonfires.
Sobs and screams echo through the cramped quarters,
Sounds of snapping bones and breaking glass blending into the reverb.
The stench of seared flesh and pepper spray
Mixes with body odor and blood.
Sirens howl in the distance, hungry to join the festivities.

Embrace the Hideous Immaculate

Little Youkai at the Witch House

(for Shigeru Mizuki)

Riding the high winds like a bed sheet flapping on a clothesline,
A ghost glides in glaucous light of a monolithic moon,
Elongated eyes shining like bright lights behind emerald glass panes.
Tombstones in the cemetery outside the old house
Smile rows of marbled teeth, rip loose of the musty, moist ground,
And clasp tiny gray hands.
They jig in a wide circle, giddy and exuberant.
Just beneath the deepest grave, an enormous furry belly jiggles.
Awakened from his dream, the Eater of the Dead bellows awkwardly
At the excitement above.
Tending to his perpetually rumbling stomach is forgotten for the moment
As he swims through packed earth like water,
Toothy maw crunching bone and dirt,
Anxious to join the reveling of his spirit brothers.
In the old house, a single eye opens in each cyclopean turret, perplexed and
puzzled, peering down at the ghoulish clamor.
Where the graveyard meets tangled, skeletal trees,
Salamander midget-men stop their feasting on the flayed flesh of a foolish traveler,
Turning blood-drenched snouts toward the laughter echoing through the forest.
Soon, dark-hunched forms, grotesque and gibbering,
Frolic within the circle of giggling stones, a multitude of merry monstrosities.
On the rooftop, a little boy bursts into laughter at his new nightmare friends.
The last tear falls, memories of a mortal childhood gratefully expelled for the night,
The dusty fate of flesh and bones only a haunting afterthought,
Buried until morning.

Chad Hensley

Exhumed

My love for her is buried
Deep in my heart
That has become a coffin
And the memory of her lies in it
A cadaver, which I dig up
Every day and make love to.

But her face will not wither
And her body will not rot
Though her eyes
Have become gleaming stones of aquamarine
That sparkle in my darkness.

Bed of Roses

My heart grows not, but undeath—
a rose garden of funeral flowers,
thick with thorns that thirst
yearning to entwine themselves
between a beautiful maid's pretty,
pale bare breasts—caress her naked body,
burying themselves.

Drinking, the thorns flourish
on the precious succulent fluid
dripping slowly from her nipples
until, like a fountain,
the nipples gush
the spouting liquid
allowing the flowers
to bloom in crimson splendor.

Once gorged,
the maid is drained.
The flowers wilt
and the garden
must return to
a plot of rich black earth
that remains moist and fresh
in a lightless place.

Chad Hensley

Lusting After Apparitions

Once I whispered
A lustful prayer after midnight
And through my open window
Flew a thin, trembling form.
Her face a pale marble
With eyes of crushed emeralds.
Long ebon locks covered
Her small bare breasts.
She smiled and embraced me.
Gazing into her eyes
I saw the reflection
Of a withering form
And I dissolved
Into the hissing wind.

Shadow Dogs

The shadow dogs run the streets
Leaping and gnashing at empty air.
Hungry for throats bared
They lunge, foaming with black froth
Refusing to bay at the sullen moon
Like common mutes chained.
Trapped in the silence between worlds
We see only the speckled darkness of empty rooms.

Midnight Snack

Outside—
Winds whip
At screen doors.
Rain splatters
From gutter rooftops.
Lightning illuminates
A pitch sky.

Inside—
Hinges shut.
Locks click.
People sleep, restlessly.

Outside—
Enormous eyes glare, searching.
Huge shadows slither, clenching.
Barred windows bend, breaking.

Inside—
Awakened faces pale.
Bones crack, crushed.
Screams fade, silenced.

Embrace the Hideous Immaculate

Storm Warning

From within the safety of the screened porch
I watched black clouds
Churn across a shadowed sky.
Torrents of pelting rain
Tore gashes in the ground.
The wind became
An incessant howl.
Hot tongues of lightning
Licked the earth.
I glanced into the clouds
Directly above my house
And, for a second, I saw
A giant pulsating eye of electricity
Gazing malignantly.
I dove into the house,
Sight a searing blur
As beneath my feet the concrete shook
And thunderous laughter echoed
In an ear-splitting roar.

Chad Hensley

Below the Waves

I wander coral-reef catacombs
Swimming deeper in black waters
With webbed feet,
My lidless eyes watching giant squids scurry
Through the mounds of tentacle eyestalks
Swaying with the currents.
I descend algae-formed stairs
Listening to the ocean's languid silence
Whisper ancient secrets.
Before an enormous sepulchre
I shout with gilled lungs.
Cold, colossal stone doors open
And I am embraced by
A multitude of tendrils.

Embrace the Hideous Immaculate

Wolfsblood II

On evening streets
residue of herd stench rises
thick with sweat and blood.

Sullen moonlight tongues
muscle and meat
casting rutting shadows.

Morning brings
Sleepless commuter crowd
Ravenous for night fall.

In late winter,
the night wakes
me early
I wander through
labyrinthine streets
Beneath eroding
towers of glass
and steel

Embrace the Hideous Immaculate

Children of the Worm

In late winter, the night wakes me early.
I wander through labyrinthine streets
Beneath eroding towers of glass and steel
Watching snow flurries on cracked asphalt.
Shuffling commuters hurry home huddled close.
I look just like them,
Trudging slowly in a heavy coat through sidewalk slush.
A short scurry through a broken grating
Leads to giant concrete sewers snaking downward.
Thick, black waters run to a fissure in a slime-coated wall.
An ancient tunnel bored out of solid earth
Descends in corkscrew spirals.
After hours, I can smell a stench stronger than human waste.
A colossal cavern grins with stalactite teeth.
Upon an underground shore,
Aquamarine waters glisten with phosphorescent seaweed.
Coiled around a gigantic stalagmite,
The white-bloated belly undulates with the tide.
A thousand pink tentacles whip the humid air, excited at my approach.
A mouth of cilia excretes in anticipation.
Disrobing, tiny eyestalks feed upon my nakedness.
I run to my mother, howling with the sadness
Of forgotten multitudes,
Assuring her that those above
Will remember one day.

Chad Hensley

Ancient One II

The night breeze hissed softly
As I awoke upon cool sands.
The light of many moons illuminated
A pathway of weathered obsidian.
Compelled, I followed staring at the stars
For I felt as if a hundred-thousand eyes
Were watching with an immense, ancient pity.
At sight's edge, I saw gigantic shadows
Moving with massive strides.
Faceless black-winged forms flew
High above me in the violet sky.
With a few steps I found myself
Before a giant mirror of unknown metal.
I screamed in utter horror
For my reflection was
A quivering mass of tendrils.

Day Dream

In the day
I dream—
A sun sets slowly
sinking into the clouds,
bleeding crimson upon them.
Naked crying children run indoors.
Inside, their mothers sit as
glistening sweet sweat
dribbles down their heaving breasts.
They stare into silver mirrors
As they touch their tender skin,
mesmerized by their beauty.

I awaken, ravenous
with thirst. Crawling up
I shall reach the moonlight
and feed on those that
dream in the night.

Chad Hensley

Dark Entry II

At twilight
I walk to the roof of my apartment
And stare over the city,
An incessant hum throbs.
If I listen carefully
I can hear a soft clicking
As a cloud of gnats swarm
Around my face.
Daddy Longlegs scamper
Over my shoes.
In every corner of the roof
Spiders spin egg sacks.
Silverfish scurry around the webs.
Roaches crawl inside the walls,
Too many to count.
I retreat to the safety of indoors.
Somehow my room seems smaller and,
Unconsciously, I can hear
A clicking in the shadows.

Embrace the Hideous Immaculate

Another Empty Midnight

She crouches within tendrils of willow limbs,
Moonlight slithering around her muddy feet.
Sapphires glitter above a smile.
With slow, quivering strides
Massive, thorned black wings unfold.
I listen to heavy flapping and soft laughter
Carried on the night wind.

Chad Hensley

Embrace the Hideous Immaculate

The Amaranth

Upon the griffin's back she sits
Bone-white hair wind-driven,
Pale face an unblemished alabaster.
Whirling, winged-fairies weave
Honeysuckle and hyacinth through her aureolin locks.
Hiding in withered woods two-headed ogres leer
Astride giant ravenous wolves,
Hungry for her affection.
They cower, covering their obsidian eyes from the porcelain moon
And creep toward her with glittering underworld gifts
In hopes of attaining her undying love.
Two tiny teeth protrude slightly
Below her smile, shadows devouring the night.

Chad Hensley

The Call

I listen to the night breathing
Under the stars.
Nocturnal cacophonies
Lull me to dream of
Sunless purple skies.
Huge monarch wings
Bath me in frigid winds.
Tremendous tentacles caress
My thin, pale form.
A thousand gaping mouths
Scream my name in a language
I should not understand.
Awakening, membranous wings
Unfold from my flesh.
Tendrils of cartilage uncoil
From my arms and legs.
Extra eyes in my stomach
See deep into space.
I shout a reply
From my chest of mouths
And go to greet my father.

Embrace the Hideous Immaculate

The Night-Child's Wardrobe

Tired of silence,
The night-child always walks
With dirty, bare claws
Scraping the cracked concrete like
Wind whipping through a window's lattice.

Appalled at imposters,
The night-child hunts
Thin, frail mortals dressed like death,
Faces caked clown-white
Pretending to be blood drinkers.

Bored with black,
The night-child wears ivory
With a splash of crimson
Ravished from pale, punctured throats
And slashed wrists torn asunder.

Chad Hensley

Hungering for Apparitions

From within the midnight shade of a leafless tree
I watch her walk across cracked, cement gravestones.
She steps delicately,
Black lace dress billowing,
An imitated emotion.
Pinned to her throat,
A strange gothic brass brooch
Glitters in livid moonlight.
Her bone-white hair
Whips around the smooth
Marbled flesh of her expressionless face
In the autumn wind.
She whispers
And I walk to her
As she spreads her arms wide.
Ice-cold lips caress my naked chest;
A twin prick of needle pain.
I shiver with chill ecstasy
As her pale skin begins to blush.
She laughs hysterically and
I awaken only to the hissing wind
Mocking me beneath a gloating moon.

Embrace the Hideous Immaculate

Phantasmagoria

Marian drops her porcelain mask
To the petaled-floor and frowns.
Reflecting a thousand pinpricks of sunrise,
Shattering pieces spin.
The morning hisses with laughter.
She whimpers
Dissolving into the woodwork.

Chad Hensley

Keep Sakes

A withered rose,
Stiff, brittle petals
Still clinging to a stem of barbed thorns,
Marks the middle of an empty diary.

Pieces of a porcelain mask reform
To reveal an expressionless face
And then shatter into razor shards.

In the flame of a melted candle
A winged imp dances
Anxious for the taste of tender flesh
Hoping to add a new trinket to the collection.

Decay

Black is my soul,
like the sockets of a skull,
empty.

Cold is my flesh,
the sun never to set upon it
shining.

Withered am I,
dried and rotting,
buried.

About the Author

A skilled reporter on cultural extremes in music and art, Bram Stoker Award-nominated author, Chad Hensley, saw several years of his writing on underground subjects published as *EsoTerra: The Journal of Extreme Culture*, through Creation Books in 2011 now available at Amazon.com.

Hensley's non-fiction has appeared in such praised publications as *Apocalypse Culture 2*, *Terrorizer*, *Spin*, *Rue Morgue*, *Hustler*, and *Juxtapoz*. He has sold short stories to the anthologies *The Darker Side: Generations of Horror*, *The Dead Inn*, *Allen Koszowski's Inhuman*, and Chad's short story collection with Wilum Pugmire, *A Clicking in the Shadows*, received an honorable mention in *Year's Best Fantasy and Horror*. His poetry has also received honorable mentions in *Year's Best Fantasy and Horror* as well as being nominated for the Science Fiction Poetry Association's Rhysling Award. His poetry appearances include the magazines *Star*Line*, *Dreams and Nightmares*, *Space and Time*, *Crypt of Cthulhu*, *Deathrealm*, and the *Chiaroscuro* website. Chad currently resides in New Orleans, Louisiana.

Publication History

"Grotesque Statue" *Amaranth #1*, 1991.

"Mortal Remains II" *Free Worlds #1*, 1994.

"At Night I Play" *Rictus #3*, 1994.

"Nocturnity" *Crossroads #4*, 1992.

"Last Embrace" *Amaranth #1*, 1991.

"Church Bizarre" *Deathrealm #9*, 1989.

"Birthright" *Dagger of the Mind #2*, 1990.

"Festival of Stigma Martyrs" *Deathrealm #13*, 1990.

"Necrotivity" *frisson #3*, 1996.

"Nocturne" *Dagger of the Mind #2*, 1990.

"Silent Brood" *Wicked Mystic #25*, 1996.

"The vampire witch boy" *Flesh & Blood #10*, 2002.

"Listen" *Rictus #4*, 1995.

"A View of Videodrone Godflesh" *Psychos*, 1992.

"Big Island Sunset" *Star*Line # 36.2*, 2013.

"Stranded in Mississippi" *Dark Legacy #15*, 2005.

"Diablo Musica" *Black October #6*, 2004.

"Mardi Gras After Midnight" *The Heliocentric Net Anthology*, 1996.

"Mexican Standoff" *Nasty Piece of Work #14*, 2000.

"The Jackpot" *The Blue Lady #4*, 1996.

"Pilgrimage" *Deathrealm #17*, 1992.

"Gautier Ghost Story" *Gothic.Net* website, April 2002.

"The Ghost of Buena Vista" *Dark Legacy #15*, 2005.

"A Nasty Encounter with Road Kill" *Nasty Piece of Work #12*, 1999.

"IQ Test" *Nasty Piece of Work #13*, 1999.

"Something My Grandfather Taught Me" *Black October #3*, 2002.

"Dark Entry" *The Silver Web #7*, 1991.

"American Dream" *Deathrealm #26*, 1995.

"Macabre II" *The Silver Web #7*, 1991.

"Harvest" *Malevolence #2*, 1996.

"Bedtime Story" *Deathrealm #12*, 1990.

"Hollywood Labyrinth before Sunset" *Malevolence #2*, 1996.

"Ancient One" *Midnight Shambler #3*, 1996.

"The Horde" *Vicious Circle #1*, 1993.

"Whisper" *Dreams and Nigthmares #45*, 1995.

"Abyssal Plain", *The Ancient Track #1*, 1998.

"Laugh of the Night Ocean" *Amaranth #1*, 1991.

"Feast of Lilith" *New Blood #5*, 1989.

"Metamorphose" *Bizarre Bazaar #92*, 1992.

"Mother Lilith" *Crypt of Cthulhu #90*, 1995.

"A Murmur of Taunting Immortiality" *Rouge Et Noir #5*, 1994.

"Nethermost Cavern" *Crypt of Cthulhu #90*, 1995.

"Initiation into the Night Forest" *Thin Ice #10*, 1991.

"Ghost of the Nucleur City" *Stygian Articles #1*, 1995.

"Waiting for Eternity" *Tales of Lovecraftian Horror #5*, 1997.

"Pains of the Sufferer" *Thin Ice #9,* 1991.

"Night Carnival" *Crossroads #4,* 1992.

"Savings and Loan" *Flesh and Blood #7*, 2001.

"Block Party" *Dark Muse* website, October 2000.

"Little Youkai at the Witch House", *What the Cacodaemon Whispered*
    chapbook Flesh & Blood Press, 2001.

"Exhumed" *Gothic.Net* website, January 2001.

"Bed of Roses" *Prisoners of the Night #3*, 1989.

"Lusting After Apparitions" *Black Lotus #4*, 1995.

"Shadow Dogs" *Crossroads #4*, 1992.

"Midnight Snack" *Dagger of the Mind #2*, 1990.

"Storm Warning" *Crossroads #5*, 1993.

"Below the Waves" *Contortions #1*, 1996.

"Wolfsblood II" *Space and Time #94*, 2001.

"Children of the Worm", *Imelod* 1998.

"Ancient One II" *The Heliocentric Net volume 4 #2*, 1995.

"Day Dream" *Deathrealm #14* 1991.

"Dark Entry II" *Malevolence #2,* 1996.

"Another Empty Midnight", *In Darkling Woods,* 1996.

"The Call" *Dagger of the Mind #2,* 1990.

"The Amaranth" *Outer Darkness* fall annual, 1995.

"The Night Child's Wardrobe" *In Darkness Eternal #3,* 1997.

"Hungering for Apparitions" *Prisoners of the Night #5,* 1991.

"Phantasmagoria" *Prisoners of the Night #7,* 1993.

"Keep Sakes" *Outer Darkness* fall annual, 1995.

CPSIA information can be obtained at www.ICGtesting.com
Printed in the USA
BVOW02s0913220514

354147BV00003B/338/P